KNIFE THROWING THROUGH SELF-HYPNOSIS

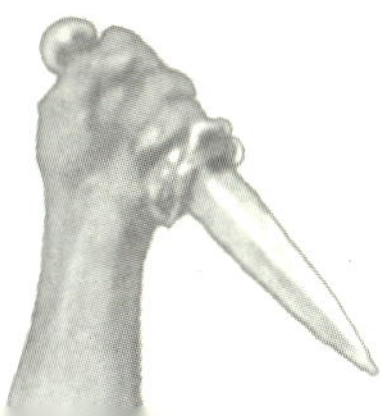

KNIFE THROWING THROUGH SELF-HYPNOSIS

POEMS

ROBIN RICHARDSON

MISFIT

MISFIT / ECW PRESS

Published by ECW Press
2120 Queen Street East, Suite 200, Toronto, Ontario, Canada M4E 1E2
416-694-3348 / info@ecwpress.com

Library and Archives Canada Cataloguing in Publication

Richardson, Robin, 1985–, author
Knife throwing through self-hypnosis : poems / Robin Richardson.

ISBN 978-1-77041-162-3 (PBK.) / 978 1 77090-435-4 (PDF) / 978-1-77090-436-1 (EPUB)

I. Title.

PS8635.I3338K65 2013   C811'.6   C2013-902489-1

Editor for the press: Michael Holmes / a misFit book
Cover and text design: Natalie Olsen, Kisscut Design
Cover image © Fotosearch
Author Photo: Nir Arieli
Printed and bound in Canada by Coach House 5 4 3 2 1

The publication of *Knife Throwing Through Self-Hypnosis* has been generously supported by the Canada Council for the Arts which last year invested $157 million to bring the arts to Canadians throughout the country, and by the Ontario Arts Council, an agency of the Government of Ontario. We also acknowledge the financial support of the Government of Canada through the Canada Book Fund for our publishing activities, and the contribution of the Government of Ontario through the Ontario Book Publishing Tax Credit and the Ontario Media Development Corporation.

'TIS THE REFUGE WE TAKE WHEN THE UNREALITY OF THE WORLD WEIGHS TOO HEAVY ON OUR TINY HEADS . . . RELAX; SINK INTO IT; YOU'RE NO BETTER THAN ANYBODY ELSE.

3.18–3.19 — *Who's Afraid of Virginia Woolf?*

CONTENTS

HOW GODS GO ON THE ROAD

She keeps a crystal ball on the coffee table
at a Super 8 somewhere between Harrodsburg,
Kentucky, and the cornfields she's afraid to enter.
She's thirty again. Spends her birthday burning
sage, rearranges history with the lifting
of a little toe, composes wars while singing
in the shower — "Viper's Drag," "Honey Dipper."
She's the "Lady with the Fan." Tan as deep
as tamarind. Whatever secrets she's received,
what talents, doors as wide as steak knives open
on a nebula she knows she'll one day enter.
Weather will not touch her, nor the sounds
of schoolboys in their march to physics. They
won't fix this hole. Alive too many lifetimes
to believe in cures, she passes decades with the gait
of Tolstoy heroines. However deep she cuts,
it is the blade that bleeds. Her skin like water
holds no form, but folds, and folds, and follows
numbly through the hours of a day.

VLAD THE UNINSPIRED

Tracking bomb threats through Bucharest, you
could have held them in your breath like folk songs,
each ignition red the way a handshake tightens

at the mention of a too-familiar name. The wars
were only whiffs of skin, new patterns on the cobble
patched with shades of summer tan.

SALEM: UNOFFICIAL TRANSCRIPT

The year her seizures became more frequent — dirtied
    bonnet too familiar with the wood and grassy patch
outside the barn — she burned her lips on chapel candles
    as if a kiss could be a prayer, could prove her innocence.
The year she found a ferret at the gate, gold-pawed, fond
    of recitation, whispered Chaucer in her ear to get a blush.
The year she broke her jaw against her father's riding crop,
    dropped daisies from a cut that split like batter.

MAYBE EVEN REALER

The cabinetmaker's daughter, while
dowsing with the Girl Guides in Muskoka,
finds a stream three feet below the bedrock.
Sun has bleached her braids, a séance
steeps her voice in mandolins so when she
speaks she seems to sing. The Girl Guides
are a loyal troop; too green to think of heat
or how the bear's skin makes him ornery.
The forest leaves its imprint on a path
where mindful girls may see the seedling
of a full-grown fern. Feeling barefoot
through the mud, they turn their beaks
towards a belt of meteors — slow-spinning
past the blue they've come to know as day.

THE SECOND COMING; I'M AFRAID OF ALMOST EVERYTHING

Toddler dunce-capped in the corner of a five-and-dime, reciting car wrecks, carving quotes from B films in the rim of a Styrofoam cup. Can't make him slur, suck thumbs like Gerber Babies. This thankless offspring swapped afterbirth for new slacks and a collared shirt. What's worse, his thirst for maple whiskey, wine mulled in grails too hearty for these new hands. Hired flower girls to serve his cause, Lolita-lipped, lean as matchsticks. Watch the hot pink way they wash his toes: our favourite show. Polanski's muse, Rosemary's second son, or something worse like nursery ghosts come back to haunt the mom that let them teethe on Chinese lead.

WHEN VACATION MEANS THE FEASTING OF THE SEA

The cruise ship's captain, after every electrical storm,
relieves himself over the starboard banister —
his contribution to the calm. He doesn't check
that no one's looking, leans in
like a porpoise at the dinette's crystal
coffee table. If the ocean is a yawn,
so nonchalant, his ship's the little hum
that keeps it gaping — paced perfectly
to carve in longitude across the whitecaps.
He imagines capsizing, tries to see his passengers
inverted: evening gown to chandelier to spiral stairs'
red velvet overhead. He thinks of Fred Astaire instead.
Ginger in a mint shawl, fawning over the ghost
of a grand piano. Sallow-faced, he sips his julep —
two cubes, blue-hued, heavy on the bourbon.

MERCUTIO
a family history

Mercutio's mother wore a red scarf to her own
beheading, neck a perfect curve before it split.
He was seven, waited while a mountain leaked
its mauve across a row of mastheads. He knew

when it hit, the way a stare is felt, or how
an ocean knows its own approaching storm.
Spent a month among brassieres, rolling
in aroma. Raided her drawers, lace became

his blanket; lush against the face in shapes
of flora. She'd been so lean, elk unburdened
by fur, never stern, giver of cocoa, lozenges
as pink as nipples, sweet and quick dissolving.

MERCUTIO
a personal history

Sure, when you were kids he may have slipped
        you in his mouth,
a favourite game. It was his naked knee, a scab

too much like cherry not to pluck. The rug
        was made of knots, worn
by loafers, thin branches broken at recess, dragged

across the surface in an hour of boredom. You
        were shy then.
Thin-limbed, lips so big you couldn't help but taste

each grain of dust, nun's fruit perfume, Romeo
        as well; what his fingers
left on a mango passed before class. Yellow.

Once, Lego lined the gap between you. Kneeling
        about the barracks.
Built a moat of blue tiles, teeth used to pry a half-inch

tree from its pedestal. As a man you told your
        history to the whores
of boardwalk mornings. Boys so fine

they passed for blades. Crashed parties, slipping
        a flea's-width
of caviar between your wisdom teeth.

HOW GODS ARE MADE – *Part Two*

A penny enters halfway up the foot and flattens.
This is the first of her armour, guard
against the snow, though semen settles
on her stomach, slips in so that her son
will have webbed fingers, and her veins
burn brightly as they draw down
blood to warm her feet. She's mute,
cherry-haired, a carnivore, she hardens
as the coins accrue, advance towards her
torso. She will not shrink, not stand
atop the mantel; trinket added to dragoons
of frontline statuettes. Instead she readies
for the charge; a shield made of braids,
bassinet of broadswords.

THORA THE PILGRIM

Bone shows through the opening of her snakebite,
        calloused foot on cool grass, naked save the rosary
of swallow beaks. Free of brick, brass work swapped
        for open air, where breeze makes braille of her forearm.
One sleep more, one plum eye widening its breadth
        'til half-blind, batlike, she paces. Lost three weeks:
she sleeps in moss, blanketed by fits of hunger
        as her gut becomes a choir, low enough to shake
the june bugs from their branches.

THORA AT THIRTEEN

She wants a ghost, or more, a pooka: horse
whose hooves lead steady to the cliff. Uneasy
'cause she can't get off on flesh alone, such stone,
those statues slack beside the crosswalk, not
fumbling, troubled, only form: heavy-ordered
in its place. In museums, dressed as a peasant,
she sketches fauna, brushes up on Roman myth,
walks Degas-like. If she were a sketch
or best a bluish streak across the canvas, barely
human, she'd be pigment, curled cobalt
in an old Picasso. She's uneven, eyes slant clockwise
and counter-clockwise, fingers keep time
like choirs on the thigh. She's antsy, licks
the paint of a Monet when no one's looking.
No one ever is.

FERAL IN KILLARNEY

Nodding off on the dock. The ocean is a shiver,
too tender for the kraken. Path of smoke, pork
on spit, which inches to an outer layer; plum sky,
she feels small, burns to litter sand with all her parts.

Been camped ten days; friend of stone, slope
to clinging mussels, which she eats. They taste
of prisms. She's underdressed, pimpled
like a turkey's dewlap. Tent is torn, ears stiff
with dried magenta where black flies bit. Hunts
pike, poised to souvenir the fins, piled neat like
china, counts days with scrapes across a pine.

She likes to be alone, packs earth inside her,
sprawls, lets the sun, ants, and beetles burrow.

INHERITANCE

My great grandmother was a chocolate model — broad
boyish silhouette, spent her time in French gowns
gathering applause. My father was a mustached Cadillac
owner, cowboy-booted, carrying a stuffed white rabbit
he called Harvey. He was crumb cake at the racetrack,
raised brows, scars thinning into anecdotes. My aunt
read tea leaves, saw a train derailed, fangs
unloaded on a swaying jowl, cigarettes and fights
by matchbook. My teacher talked of chalk-drawn
backward letters on a blackboard, astronomy's retro
T-shirt: Orion hunched over February skies, Jack
London's dogfights, crayon drawn lightly over maps
of Yellowknife, and cold cremations.

MIKE KOOH'S PALLIATIVE CARE UNIT

The scene where she slips a koi into a patient's colostomy bag
just to see if something can take more shit than she can
— is particularly disquieting.

Three clicks from flatline he mastered necromancy. Neon
from the all-night deli gawking through gauze curtains
as a pause between two beats became a birth date. Nurse

entered in a fern-patterned frock, thermos spiked
with brandy, brandishing a scalpel. She held his oxygen
in the palm of her body, pacing 'til his strength regained.

She carved a flock of buzzards in his forearm, tickled by
the way he flinched in afterthought, caught his breath in vials
wide enough to fill a lung in case he fixed to die a second time.

THE FUTURE SHOULD NOT BE SHARED

A clairvoyant caregiver dips her fingers
in the palm of an aging ballerina. She charts
the skid marks on her leotard; legs of twine
once twisted in a waltz of soldiers, now

resigned to pacing, pink-slippered
on a mismatched marble floor. She sits
aplomb, back exact as starched lace,
shawl shoulder-slipping, folds revealing

moles in ominous configurations. Clairvoyant
slaps a photograph against the ashtray,
tattered two-page spread, Swan Lake, long-
necked congregation. *Past*, she says. *Present*

is the chipped-knee, crow's feet, square
tableau of kitsch and kitchen table. *Future*
falls between them; figures coming through
the curtain of an open window stand in tandem

with the spider plants and plaques in scrawl
against the far wall. Five men. Five chiming
in a ghostlike choir where a love affair
becomes a pulp-book, plotted perfectly to end.

TERTIARY CHARACTERS: A BEHEADING

All axes hold a half-moon as they lift aligned
with felon necks. Cheek to stone, wave
to grid (cartographer's stippling so the ships
leave wakes of ink). Hooded in burlap, a man

stands. *Callous*, he thinks, *gravity*. He lifts his arms,
adjusting grip. *Is it sharp enough?* He swings. Thirty-two.
Boots polished twice to hide the splay. Clumped
lace, straps of ocean salt. His wife rubs words

from his feet, where *please* and *please* and also prayers
to let the head fall gentle to the pit. Simple. Rag to
wipe the blade. Now dragging self through field,
home, he comes to supper with a grateful bow.

USING LINE TO MEASURE WEIRDNESS

A whore's account of ivory

The 1800s

Stampede bleeding through the gullet when he sneezes

Tusks that lean like dancer's feet towards the carving knife

The sculptor is a narcoleptic

Dreams of peeling back his hands

Sees fingers as piano keys

Femur whittled to a soap dish, vine and cherub

Or her hairpin, hot with histories of sand

Sharp enough to cut the fringe that hides her furrow

ADRIATIC DAYBREAK

A gondola palms the water: idle heron,
half sunk toe dipped periodic by an adolescent.
He bribes the gondolier with heirlooms, dictates
with his gait the oar's ascension. Varnished oak
on open air, barely touching down. He hones
a breeze, glows to think of far-off docks.

ONLY FOOLS TELL SECRETS INDOORS

Horizon lanced through rouge on Booth Lake. Jennie
at the deck in her nightdress, straps to cover bruises
big as Red Rose figurines. She thumbs them where

the dress comes satin-cornered to her shoulder. Folding
thoughts like linen in a drawer too mint to make her bitter —
how a house becomes a man, becomes a husband. Every log

a lifetime, fog caught coiling in the kitchen sink, pink stains
of boiled rhubarb, blood. A book on how to quell a ghost.
Three years she's lived alone, sleep-scuffling, scarring,

wrestling with the sheets. He will not let her sleep; three
shades of ivory; how he glows when he's aroused, surrounds
her as a man without a body bangs against the gate.

THE PILOT OF FLIGHT 146

The mist you are seeing
is caused by a difference
in temperature.

The temperature outside
is different from
the temperature inside.

Once we close the door
and prepare for takeoff,
the mist will disappear,

which will make us
very sad, because
we like mist.

BASS ENTERPRISE: HOW GOSSIP GIRL CAUGHT THE DEVIL

Real-estate mogul thrown from high-rise
by a shadow dipped in city lights the way
a kid dips sticks of glue in glitter, makes a wand.

His widow speaks so highly of the spilled wine
as it spreads in Rorschach on her sequins; see
Caligula, his boner buried in assassin's knives,

a casket carried by that last, charitable crack
of thunder. He will not be missed. His kiss of cold
cigars and gold keys clanking at the locks

of her autonomy. He wore no horns but pawed
the ashes of his adversaries. They called him green lynx
for the poise, the lean, black reach of his ambition.

You must know spiders cannibalize. When quarantined
they feast in heaves of leg and tooth until
the last emerges fat and peckish still. He was as fat

and peckish when he died as when he sold
handguns to disgruntled lunch-men at his stepson's
high school. Some say he knew the target.

In a tweed tie, seven thousand dollar Dolce & Gabbana
three-piece he lies unwrapped on a slab of street;
his spirit haggling with an Upper East Side bird-lady

for solace in her gut until he's strong enough again to plot.

NAY, IT IS; I KNOW NOT "SEEMS."

King Hamlet, in a blue-lit suit, mistook my bedroom
for a Denmark terrace. Between nightstand and
a stack of books he stood tap-tapping a cane of soot.
Lamp-lit nostrils flaring so I had to squint, dusted
brow-ridge, garden boots, a glow the likes of slow-
approaching Neptunes. He'd been napping when
it happened, thinking, half aflame, of panties —
satin on the headboard, heedless of the queen. He
followed foot to carpet, fray to wood, and tripped.

BOLD IN THE EVENING

He leans towards the skyline, shies away
from silence: when the jukebox stops he hums.
Chaste barman in his too-tight trousers, tinted
cowlick. He rubs against the stool, steady lift
towards the light above the sink. He's thinking
of a car-wreck, wastes the day in hubcaps
at the crux of overdrinking.

PORN STAR ON MONDAY MORNING

The mole that itches at her hip bone barely shows.
She bends her knees unshaved, sits spread-eagle
like the camera is a thoroughbred. Behind her: pale
plaster, lamp, an unlocked door. But watch, when
she disrobes there is a flea half-frantic at the outskirts
of her girlish gaze.

ABANDONED MANNEQUIN PLANT

There are five hundred states of sky.
Cliffs stripped bare by breeze reveal

themselves in rungs of pebble soldiers
up their sides. I want to join them.

Torso twisted at the window where
each pane is made of spray paint, broken

glass and times past. I am static, stuck
in fiberglass and plaster, asking for the star

that found Geppetto.

HIGHWAYHEAD'S GUIDE TO GIRLS WITH OVERBITES

titled after Terrance Hayes

If she's shaking, if she's point-toed in a corner jigging,
    don't advance. Thumb the cleavage, chain-link thing
she's wearing at the Waffle House. Don't fumble your hellos.
    It's only 8 p.m. and you can taste her growing anxious.
If the echo is despondent, hunchbacked at a pot,
    it's that she sees your face. You're telling, downcast,
can't connect her freckles though you've seen them reconfigure
    in the neon *all night*, typed cursive on her fingers, cotton
drawstringed waist. She's not a liar. If she reaches for your sleeve
    across the counter it means *hold me*. Take her Bic-scrawl
for river dips, hips for rowing. Watch her sun her lisp
    in lifting mantras: *omelette*, *onion*, *orphaned coat*, or *notepad*.

If you see her reach for shift, her apron up still further,
    forward leaning, tell her that you mean to keep her.

DISCO AT THE END OF DAYS

Saints go screeching down the underpass.
Black cloaks against the snow; they move like
phosphenes resurrected from the rubbed eye
of a diabolist. Barbed gods gurgling
at the turnstiles. Shiny, fashionable; they walk
as if the roads were runways, shredding
to confetti as they tangle briefly in the wheels
of a transport truck from Cincinnati. Now
the Northern Lights touch down to torch
what's left of us: a misty green-lipped kiss.
The gods go ape-shit at the flame, the way
a dance floor takes to cheering
at the onset of a latest hit.

THE LEOPARD SOCIETY

The skin he claimed as his own
Black spots vast as red dwarfs
Orange like looking through a flame-lit finger
How he followed her through fields grown on old bones
Calves are best, or knees, for eating
Throat torn, moping in a palm disguised as paw
He brought her kicking through the coals
Each feast a fellow tribesman

NEW GENERAL THEORY OF THE GOLD-EYED ALBINO

We pushed beyond dance, hugging
to a waltz, sleeping in the weeds. He smelled
of static like the foil wrap around a chocolate
egg. Plucking bruises zinc and crescent
as the moon's rude slap, picking winkles
from their shells he fell into a trance. To know
an earthquake watch his eyelids as he dreams,
dismissing myth in favour of the radio's grey buzz.

He's been alive too long, lightning grinding up
against him at a beach bash in the east of Spain.
We drank too much to notice how he glowed
thereafter; pink vines riding up his forearm
like a cheap tattoo. No touching. Now a field
froths with old bones pushing up to mimic snow.

He knows because he watched the soldiers
sinking through the green with clotted swords.
Had to let it happen; all those meteors just
itching to unload on overcrowded continents.
He speaks slow in old vernacular, regresses
when we kiss — my lips a crust beneath his touch.

Next stop: Sixtieth Street, transfer
to the four, five, six, or the N/R.
Sixtieth Street and Bloomingdale's,
next stop . . .

Hi, everyone — I'd like to take this
red light to thank you for joining us
on this, the one hundred and fifteenth
run of the M103 bus.

Now, I know some of you have
had bad days at school, work,
church, et cetera, but please don't
bring that home to your loved ones.

Leave all your stress on the bus,
and I'll toss it into the East River
when we pass it.

Bye, Baby Bunting,
father's gone a-wheeling
through the Western
dives; bronze pocket-
watch to crown a stack
of poker chips. He listens
to the breathing of each
bluffer. Even masters
have a tell.

A cat came fiddling
from the stone steps
of an ossuary
on New Year's Eve.
She sang a shanty —
how the rats rose up
like phoenix-things
the day the ship
burned off the coast
of Peggy's Cove.

LITTLE ROBIN EXPLAINS GROWING UP

I did a lot to be human: small and ratty
        mass of girl gut-aching through an April.
Thought it was an ulcer. What does static
        on pink cotton have to do with sleep?
Soundly on I kept my growling to the teeth.
        Too grisly for this kindergarten nap: grindstone,
calico's split pelvis in the grass. I saw it happen —
        hidden in a crayon, still can't write it — fits
of finding out about the bomb, caldera,
        how a cell can kill its neighbours. I lost his love
the day I learned to know things on my own.

YASMIN

Every time you sneeze there is another bomber on the news
	brought groveling to the knees of virgins. You can see him
minced above the anchorwoman's unmovable updo. He's a cherub:
	arrow anthraxed, pointed at the air duct of a subway train.
On a flight

to Heathrow, dull with sleeping pills, I dreamed the plane had filled
	with squealing babies, each one gifted with a loaded gun to chew
while teething. See the desert with its pilgrims specked on a satellite's
	new imaging? Camels carry prophecies inside their humps. Chop
one clean across the bottom: blue means peace, red means A-bombs

	flicker in the sky like fall leaves. Sleep easy, babe. The playground
proves we reincarnate: clay on rubber on the wooden swing imagined
	as a life raft. That's your daughter with the asthma, wrapping gum
around a chain-link, saving up for World War Three.

MONTE CARLO, MISSISSAUGA

Synesthesia keeps my honorary uncle
focused on the game; four is Merlot, nine
the dentin on his mentor's molars.

A game of pool's the way
I first learned to look a good
curve straight on, watched
my uncle's oak-skinned opposition

sitting coked-up at the barstool,
steadied by the slow hoist of a cue
as he stood to take his shot. Green
was the sound of a hustle, cueball

hop-scotched across a string
of solids, sunk for five grand.
Two years old and barely tall
enough to reach the rail when

I learned to rack. They said
my mother was a shark. She kept
my teeth in jade containers. Jade
and mean was how she played.

REFLECTIVE SURFACES

On the subway I imagine
rural husbands hollowing
a well with silver spoons. Pink
rope around their waists,
like ribbon. Thirty feet down
and you can see the stars
at noon. Dozing now I almost
drool. Just imagine as they
take a bucket to their feet to fill
with satellites and Hudson water.

TRILLIUM

The hospital is pleasant enough: clean sheets,
plush clown nodding from the nightstand.
There's a woman in the hall who says she hears
her heart rate in another patient's room, believes
he stole it while she slept. A laundry bin sits
brimming by my door with scrubs of bleach
and brine. Its scent of dirty crotch can't pull
me from these morphine dreams. My broken
arm, a python swimming through the bright lights
of an operating table. My doctor wore a gold-
chained *S* around her neck, or was it lightning
squirming past her sternum? Waking up half-
drugged is fun enough when phantoms from
the third floor smuggle out between the teeth.

KNIFE THROWING THROUGH SELF-HYPNOSIS

To pass as a strong man, move boulders through
inflated pores, black lumps stiff as good scotch. Watch
the rolling of your *R*s, too often soft, unworthy of the
buckle's brass eagle just above the cock. The cock

is paramount. No hero hides his bulge — blue worming up
the thigh like high-wires. It's not enough to fuck
the daughter of a dragon, her claws gone through your
waist. You must undo whatever noble airs she claims,
maintain your status with the slitting of a tooth-white throat.

LUCKY NUMBERS

Spent November weathering the flicker
        of a sitcom; spiced rum smooth like swallowing

an ex-wife's offhanded compliments.
        It wasn't all bad all the time. It wasn't bad at all. His little girl

in her karate *gi*, one hundred sit-ups at his feet.
        He'd taught her how to bluff, to look a straight flush

straight on, aces for eyes, and smile. Find a child who's not born
        a little scared. I dreamed of earthquakes. While I curled up

like dirty laundry in the den, my father fretted over gambling
        debts. He never meant to walk off when I broke

my arm; a misdirected back-flip in the backyard;
        it just happened.

DONOR

Enemy with my face, kidneys bright
        as boysenberry, sneezing while they swing
my skeleton on iron rigs. You med-school
        slacker prodding at the holes I have for eyes,
tipsy on formaldehyde. I'm afraid they'll
        give my heart to the kid in room six — jolt
too hard against his warbler ribs. Signed
        my donor card at thirteen, thinking I'd be
pillaged in my sleep; every beat another rung
        up in the queue. The coolers prepped
and stacked unlabelled, surgeons pacing,
        pagers quiet while I keep these organs warm.

THE MASONIC LODGE

Robbing graves for ball gowns
somewhere between the sawgrass
and a bomb-bellied toad, we stopped
to dig our heels in the snow. You
were alive then, taupe-eyed punk
with plastic bangles, blue braids
wound tightly in the ringlets you
would credit to your father's 'fro:
his marijuana in your bra, our bodies
plump with Rockets, curly fries, chocolate
from the five-and-dime. We danced
like seizures, sucked our fingers
salt-dry, rocking homeward on the
blue-lit, late-night Streetsville bus.

IF HE TOOK ME

In a basement made of bombshells — some flesh.
  In velvet paintings, black-lit, mushrooms patterned
by protractor. In a sheet fort, ghost-robed five-
  year-old with holes for eyes, gone stumbling into traffic.
In the market, gourds like swoop-necked geese
  around our ritual. If he took me in red dirt, Chelsea
mornings, in a wind of insects, white gloves, biographies.
  In Troy, in sword fights, cameras making pixels
of our fixed stares. In tin canoes, loose threads
  to tread our knuckles. If he took me in a haunted house,
Niagara Falls, in Ferris wheels filled with dread. In brown
  boots, bars, in bottles of Ouzo, studious as schoolgirls.
In autumn, jobless, watching Lynch films. In a rabbit
  hat, pumpkin plush around his shoulders, skin
inside, asleep five hours. In a dream of beating, bruised
  knee, in love with freckles new formed on a too-sunned
cheek. In books, in wing-stubbed shoulder blades, my
  ripped wig, his fists so Greek the way they marble
clean against the sheet.

RANAVALONA

I'd have my slave play preludes
on a toy piano, each wrong note
equates a slap, leaves pink so neon
you could see it from the street.

He would sleep beneath my bed
with box springs drilling gently
through his dreams. I'd have him
breed with Japanese game show girls,

their giggles backdropping fellatio.
I'd have him pray to gods made
of spaghetti, give him mints, warm
weather when he's good, would

strip him down to the wit he keeps
reserved for cocktails, watch him
pee. He'd be a blond; bronze
shouldered he would sniff my feet

beneath a canopy of snake weave.
I would record his syrup-breath, and
widow's peak. So sweet the way
he sneaks out Sundays to the diner,

drowns in malt and discount waffles.
He doesn't want to be alone, roams
outside my bedroom brooding over
notions of a picket fence.

I'd have him dance by orange light,
lick cayenne from my thigh, would
quell his spirits with a leer so loathing
he'd forget where he was from.

PORTRAIT IN TRANSLUCENT INK

I'd scratch my calves through the bone
if left too long to my own devices. There
are faces on the stage that look like bullets
if you squint. I think so much about
the bloodshed of a battement, those leotards
gone ripping through the quick lift
of a broken toe. It sucks to know so much
about a craft. The static on the screen means
stars are fritzing, fingering their astronauts
like pint-sized pets. Pretend the world
is round, at least for now I'd like to roll
back where I came from; curled
in a laundry bin beside my parents' vintage
ashtray stand. An unabashed yawn, hands
the size of spiders, pulling threads through
buttonholes to web around a thumb until
plump and numb.

THE GAFFER

Would need to manoeuvre
through these streets, chic plot,
it's not as if the focus

shifted. So clear it nearly
splits a freckle, lifts beige
to bronze and polishes.

This is where the eye goes.

Collapsible face forgot
to keep its purpose. Now a lip
and lightly dimpled chin.

Dialogue is useless.
In this film
there is only the freckle.

ELIZABETH TAYLOR IN THE SANDPIPER

The instance in which a young girl
refines her trade: cleanliness, small
ridges at the upper lip, soliciting each
summer guest to take his chances
with the mouth. Herself a circumstance
of hip, mist-breathed, baking fowl

the way a butcher breaks his bread, with
humour. Made to wear, her pleated slacks
beige, she wipes her palms with sour mash,
mistakes a *thank you* for a gentle slap.

OBVIOUSLY, DOCTOR, YOU'VE NEVER BEEN A TWELVE-YEAR-OLD GIRL
— The Virgin Suicides

Punch bowl of coconut, pulp
        piñata still intact. She taps it
as she passes. Red circumference,
        crudely copied 6 a.m. cartoon.
She sees herself in strong rope
        swinging from the rafters — still
intact. Her sisters lean against
        the railing, fingering their fists
as if a palm could feel the fantasy
        of squid and stout conquistador.

**OF COURSE HE HAS A KNIFE. WE ALL HAVE KNIVES.
IT'S 1183 AND WE'RE BARBARIANS.**
— ***The Lion in Winter***

Stay skinny to avoid being eaten
by your king. If you bleed you leak
the ocean's dirty secrets; dolphins

gang-raped, whales giving up their sperm
to harpoon-bearing mariners.
Your teeth are showing, dandelion-crown

goes rotten in your braids the day
you strayed — a solar flare, a few new
freckles traceable above the clavicle

make schoolboys shudder. Damn
you're a looker, lucky to be born
in times when thighs are not an entrée.

Wrapped in his jacket of dust a crocodile goes ticking
beneath the floorboards. His loose tooth a first mate's future

spade. Wendy huddles snug above, nipples soldier-straight,
chafed where wool is rubbed too tight by the collar.

A thimble's-worth of semen spotting at the chin. Again
she let him in. Again he left his shadow loitering

amongst the labels in her dresser. Whether six or three
a week he circles summoned by her Ouija board. A boy

so lost he lingers at the gate, awaits each after-midnight
sheet-fort congregation — Wendy, her teddies, and him.

IT LOOKS FAKE, I LIKE IT
—Joe Versus the Volcano

I want to get married at the mouth
of a volcano before jumping in.
It's the sort of wish girls have in grade
school when they see their teacher
linger at the sidewalk with a hickey
passing as a birthmark. Okay maybe
they don't. I did. Once I saw my father
touch the gemstoned ear of a woman
at the store. He called her *Calla Lily*,
brought her a lampshade landscaped
with the island of Waponi Woo.

BETTE DAVIS, BLINDED BY A FLEA-SIZED NEBULA, RESUMES HER ROLE LIKE THE OLD PRO THAT SHE IS

Steak on the table, framed from far away
so every evening gown can claim its cameo.

SCENES FROM THE SPOKE CLUB

The Texan in the cream tuxedo
dances slow the way a flood
upturns his family plot. A kerchief
at his collar splits him open,
smells of bacon
to the blond barista on his arm.

A zebra's bust, pried loose from
its plaque lands jaw-first
on a dozing dishboy.

Cadmium curves across a triptych,
veined in gold leaf. Up close
the painting is a timeline:
how long it takes to move
from violet to the half-moon
of a mare's neck as she rears
in tandem with her rider's spear.

E.B. FARNUM
—*Deadwood*

No more drunk than doubled over in a top hat.
    Was that the widow come to mock my dedication
to The Gem: its peepholes, gallstones, whores,
    and watered whiskey? Pink collared, I, pink blossom
of a Lichtenberg scar across my gut, a glut for flaring
    ripe with gas. What's past is past so please just
slide the key in when you leave. The arsonist inside
    me makes a move for every creaking plank but
doesn't act. Mules are fucking on the path,
    a gambler in his knickers flicking ashes at a game
of craps. Damn this coiling steam, the misty grit
    that rises from my rock glass. I'm no king but
wag my tongue just fair enough, and scheme
    so when the shit hits I'll be covered.

JERRY SPRINGER: COLOUR CHART

A man hides Smarties in his pocket.

They melt in the heat of the spotlight.

When he takes his hand out to flash the middle finger
there's a rainbow.

I'd lick it off if I were there.

His girlfriend wipes bright blue powder from her eyes when
she cries.

His mother wears tangerine with purple slacks, too fat for just
one chair.

Jerry stands to the right — skin brown as tans through string
bikinis.

WHITE HEAT

Making out with Madonna in the back of my father's Cadillac,
Mineola Elementary banner bowing overhead; pale

as our just bleached mushroom cuts. She finds a pistol in the glovebox,
squeezes with a match-thin finger so the morning moves

a little faster; fast the way our tape deck speeds past earworms
as we scan for something new. Her belly is so flat. Her laugh

is driving grade-two girls to lose their cool, undo the latches
on their insect traps. There is an earthworm in her skirt's hem.

There is a patch of grass below the dash that warms her teal-
painted toes. She knows so much. She knows we're in a time machine

so when I crack the door to leave it's night, and she's an old song
crackling through the FM of my Ford Crusader.

PRINCESS LEIA TO A LOVESICK STORMTROOPER

That swashbuckler was my downfall.
I wrapped myself around his stuck-up
bootlaces and now I'm lost.
Should have paid more attention
when I passed you in the crawl space.

LICKSPITTLE

I am the only free man.

Klaus Kinski ate his guard's last Lucky Strike,
stood naked where a fog coiled rouge around
barbed wire. He is the child's hands dropped,
bronze around the edges. Son of fields.
Uncut hair of detainees, reciting Oscar Wilde
in a plum kimono while the guards give hand jobs.
Growing among Germans, as British, as the gothic
film sets of Romania. Which are now the silent
grey and black of small screens. With reverence
I'll wash his callouses, scars too dark to be
the work of blades or jungle floors. He sweats
like storm clouds, ashes scattered in the South
Pacific. He's the harbour's parched crustaceans,
nude Namibian in his arms, his colonel's hat,
hands like armies making mince of every lock
he comes across. It's easy to comply without
the madness that makes every day a cameo.

SPACE MUTINY

The world is flat.
We know because
our paper boats go
burning off the pond
in Central Park.
Sails puffed like
extras' bonnets
in an episode of
Road to Avonlea.
I keep forgetting
where I'm from.
Three hundred feet
before the drop
becomes a storage space
for unused props.

Silly little lifespan only good for growing old. Record the facts, she says: We swam the Thames. I am the only one to do it — girl of thirty, flirting with the cabbie, say he looked like Goya, ate me out beside the entrance of a Marks & Spencer, bobble-headed Hawaiian eying from the dash.

I was a teacher for a week — boys of thirteen diddling on while I talked dirty about colonial history. Had enough? I grew up in a weathered prom dress circa '86, spent half a lifetime growing tits. Sleeves are soaked in heart, sleeps are ever-wrapped in wanting never to wake up. My sponsor is a monster.

Yoga course in Goa just to be; I had forgotten how to breathe. These maps for hands, how many lines it takes to make my psychic aunt insist I'll live forever. Several thousand sleeps from being human, chatting with a pint of amber. But I'm blond, I say. Swear I'll never suck that pint, that man again.

My gin is sleepy, says it needs to dance for money. I make big boys buckle in the black light of a haunted hole, this blemished stretch of Yonge Street. Fact: I am the kindest face to kick *The Canterbury Tales* off your table. Don't want to be your muse but if I must, just know the record's never real.

VERTIGO

Crystal wall all amber and decanter
        makes a porthole of this bistro.

I dine alone. I know
        when William Shatner beams through tanked

on mad cow, he'll come true
        to me. The marquee spelling out our union:

Terror at 20,000. The ticket booth
        attendant steadies on the ladder's dented rung.

I lose the plot too often, thought
        she slipped; that sidewalk waiting six feet

beneath her sneakers.

MADDY JOE FROM PORT CREDIT ROAD

We listened
from a playroom
in the basement
as her father's liver failed.

How he'd raged
against the unclean
towel, toppled
cold as his last beer.

WHEREVER WE ARE

Where fire matches radio reception — fuzz
 for fuzz, where fog's our largest export; forty klicks

from Barret's Drugs & Co, slow buildup
 to a shipwreck. All our postcards feature slit masts

hoisted in the bay like widows waving in their long-
 sleeved canvas nighties. I can't sleep without the CBC

on, need a voice like Jimmy Stewart's speaking through
 the hush of salt-pocked windows, watching with held

breath. I love the candle going out before we fall
 asleep. I love the way my back feels when it's turned

towards you with new freckles formed like meteors.
 You wash yourself in Epsom salts while reading

captains' logs compulsively. Off-season we have come
 to watch this snow globe town go empty as its church bells

break into a slow dance with the salt breeze. I need
 you just the way you work reclined while winter storms

perform outside our window, whistling for a page to play with
 as they lull down to a mist.

BROWNIES ARE BEST FRIENDS FOREVER

Lana joined me on her parents' pullout couch
the night of our sleepover. Her Gap Kids catalogue
face an inch away when she said *we were made for fondling.*

That night I thought I saw the roof lift off,
some grizzly god, all incest and intention,
flipped a switch and out went summer.

I've got something in my pocket, it belongs across my face.
I keep it very close at hand, in a most convenient place.
I'm sure you couldn't guess it if you guessed a long, long while.
So I'll take it out and put it on, it's a Great Big Brownie Smile!

IF MY CHILDREN

Bright red Band-Aids peeled off
        before bed, before the bright
red uncensorable nightmares, rosy
        with the glow of salmonella.

I'd drink too much, eat
        all the chocolate in their Advent
calendars then think of headlines:

        unmanned helmets on the highway,
head-first dive into the shallow end
        by accident. They'd be dyslexic
in the best case, gifted at worst,
        perverts circling the parking lot

past sundown. Shame we hardly see
        the half moon just shy
of the window's frame.

ON GUILT

She told it to the trees
trees were cut for lumber
lumber got bought
got made into a fiddle
fiddle played it to the world

I DIG MY ROCK BOTTOMNESS: A HOLIDAY POEM

I'm glancing cross-eyed at Christmas light; a cableknit clad
grizzly wheezing in her white pine grotto. I keep thinking

we should role-play: you be Santa, I'm the displaced Oompa-
Loompa with a dirty mouth. I like your knee. I like it when

you use my pillow for a paunch; red velvet, black straps
so thick they barely fit my neck. I get antsy when it's cold,

make gingerbread men dance above the stove before we bite
their heads off. I'm so quick to come apart. Repeat:

They're make-believe. They're make-believe. They're making
faces at the fishermen who dance home drunk on Mondays.

I'm not senseless. I'm a pot of coffee lulling us to life when
bored between September and a snowstorm strong as shit luck.

It's the peace that keeps me fretting, feeling up the creases
in your chest for tumours just in case, your new white hairs

as pure as kittens curling at your chin. My sinful other half
in hibernation, facing life for bad behaviour on ideal afternoons.

ALL ABOUT EVE

When Margo Channing changed
into her naked body somewhere
off screen, surrounded by men
who couldn't be bothered to look,
the world changed with her.

SECOND ANNUAL SYMPOSIUM OF INDIGNITY

The lobster with its boiled glow knows
nothing of the hostess by its tank. Her
first grey caught in lip gloss as she shows
a schizophrenic to his usual booth. She's
twice divorced, cavorting with a chef
who harbours syphilis, or was it Lyme's? A tick
caught in the elastic of his Calvin Kleins.

There's a ghost in the Ladies' Room — Thai
businessman with bullet holes for buttons.
Still the hallways smell of sulphur, servers
lose their footing at the stairs where once
sat prisoners of turf wars. Such are the hazards
of old buildings. The hostess fingers her
splintered podium, a hickey hidden
in the tangle of her multicoloured fish scarf.

MY VOICE, IN MY MOUTH

I want to get close to a lion, which sucks because the only way I know of getting close to a lion is to let him eat me. Each inch he takes will bring me closer to my goal weight. He'd paw my petticoat aside, tell lies. A daydream in the oncologist's waiting room; calm as a hyena in holding before supper. Supple janitor insists the syringe isn't his. Tread marks up his arm resemble ink rings of a rained-on postcard. I think the magazines have SARS. Boy beside me — otter-anxious — swings his legs beneath the seat as if such swinging could out-squirm leukemia. Look where the flatscreen frames our favourite terrorist all warm-eyed in his soft-serve turban. He's so handsome, trumps my lion, who is arched gymnastic at the check-in, flirting with a nurse in zebra scrubs. Her skin sheened in sanitizer. I'll don my dead aunt's wig, Obama's desert wrap, or wizard's cap. This planet is a slacker: pass sun, collect two hundred awkward interactions. Fact is we're an itch and gone as quick. Our sleeps each studded with a constellation burned out bright as myth.

ACKNOWLEDGEMENTS

I would like to acknowledge the publications in which early versions of some of these poems originally appeared:

Tin House, *Arc*, *Vallum*, *The Malahat Review*, *Acrobat*, *Qwerty*, *Fiddleback*, *The Boiler Journal*, *The Literary Review of Canada*, *The Associative Press*, *CanLit*, *Forget*, *Unsaid*, *Joyland Poetry*, *The Fiddlehead*, and *The Rusty Toque*.

Special thanks are due to the following individuals:

Michael Holmes, Emily Schultz, Thomas Lux, Kevin Pilkington, Jeffrey McDaniel, David McGimpsey, Matthew Dickman, and Sean Stanley.

This book was completed with the support of the Ontario Arts Council, the Toronto Arts Council, the Canada Council for the Arts, and the Writers' Reserve Program at the Ontario Arts Council, for which I am extremely grateful.

NOTES

"How Gods Go on the Road": "Viper's Drag" and "Honey Dipper" are Cab Calloway song titles.

"Thora the Pilgrim," "Thora at Thirteen," and "Feral in Killarney" are all selections from my long poem-in-progress "The Life and Times of Dzoavits the Volcano Dweller."

"Mike Kooh's Palliative Care Unit": "*The scene where she slips a koi into a patient's colostomy bag /just to see if something can take more shit than she can / — is particularly disquieting*" is taken from an email from my friend Mike Kooh. I've changed the name of the fish in the original message from a carp to a koi.

"Using Line to Measure Weirdness": I took the title from something a fellow student said about her work in Matthea Harvey's poetry workshop 2011, Sarah Lawrence College.

"Only Fools Tell Secrets Indoors": Taken from one of Angela Sweeting's Facebook status updates.

"The Pilot of Flight 146" and "Overheard in New York" are found poems from the website Overheardinnewyork.com.

"Nay, It Is; I Know Not 'Seems.'": The title is a quote from Shakespeare's *Hamlet*.

"Highwayhead's Guide to Girls with Overbites": The title is based on Terrence Hayes' "Lighthead's Guide to the Galaxy."

"Obviously, Doctor, You've Never Been a Twelve-Year-Old Girl": The title is a direct quote from the film *The Virgin Suicides*.

"Of Course He Has a Knife. We All Have Knives. It's 1183 and We're Barbarians.": The title is a direct quote from *The Lion in Winter*.

"It Looks Fake, I Like It": The title is a direct quote from *Joe Versus the Volcano*.

"White Heat": The poem shares a title with a Madonna song.

"Lickspittle": "*I am the only free man*" is a quote from *Doctor Zhivago*.

"Space Mutiny": The title is taken from the film *Space Mutiny* as released by *Mystery Science Theater 3000*.

"Brownies Are Best Friends Forever": The italicized final verse is taken directly from "Brownie Smile Song."

"All About Eve": The poem is titled after the film *All About Eve*.

"My Voice, in My Mouth": The title is a direct quote from the Elizabeth Bishop poem "In the Waiting Room."